CONTE

PARTICLES

FORCES

ENERGY

Letts

Natalie King • Sarah Wyatt
Tom Kendall

Red Hot Websites Science

11–14

CONTENTS

CELLS

INTERDEPENDENCE

REVISION

PREFACE

'What we learn with pleasure we never forget' – Alfred Mercier.

Most of these websites are a lot of fun with games, quizzes, animation, and sound effects. I hope you enjoy using them as much as we have.

Enjoy!

Natalie King, Sarah Wyatt and Tom Kendall

Thanks

Thanks go out to all our friends and family who have supported us in this exciting project, especially to Delroy King for letting me constantly 'hog' the computer and for all your encouragement. Plus a mention to 'bump' who actually seemed to enjoy the hum of the computer.

Thanks also to Rev. Adrian Heath and Veronica Heath for all their support and enthusiasm.

Our gratitude also to David and Assa Kendall for all their help and interest.

Thanks also to all the young people who have reviewed websites for us. Your comments and feedback were invaluable. Special thanks go to Joseph Hatton, Emily Hatton, and Daniel Lattimer.

www.kidshealth.org

Click on **Enter Kids**, then **Staying Healthy**, then scroll down to **Learning About Proteins, Carbohydrates, Calories And Fat**.

There is useful information here about the main food groups, where we can find them and why we need them. This website is fun, colourful and easy to use. Have a look at **All About What Vitamins And Minerals Do** and **Eating For Sport** which contains good advice. **The Game Closet** is a must and there are lots of yummy recipes for you to make.

You should know the seven parts to a healthy diet and be able to give examples for each. You should know what each part is for.

www.nutrition.org.uk

I liked **What's Puke?**, **What's A Fart?** and **Why Does Eating Ice Cream Give Me Headache?** from **Kids Talk**. It's the stuff teachers don't always tell you.

www.sciencenet.org.uk/database/bio/biosublist.html

Click on **Food And Digestion**, then **What Does A Balanced Diet Mean?**.

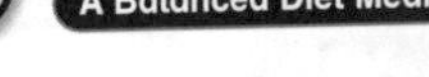

There are good facts and diagrams here about digestion. This is a great website, which answers hundreds of questions like 'Why do we produce faeces every day?'

Have a look at the rickets photograph accessed from the main **Food And Digestion** page. This shows what the disease did to young children's bones. Teachers often set research homework on rickets. It's often hard to find good pictures as it's almost unheard of these days due to better nutrition.

www.nutrition.org.uk
Go to the secondary education section.

What Makes Farts Smell is a wicked section under **Food And Digestion**. It says you really shouldn't try to light these. Find out why!

www.nutrition.org.uk

Click on **Education**, then **Secondary**, then **Digestion**, and finally **What Are The Main Stages Of Digestion And Absorption?**.

There is some good information about digestion here but it is bordering on GCSE standard. Remember, digestion is about chopping up food so it's small enough to get through the gut wall and into the blood.

Click on **Digestion Questions** for a series of test questions to see what you can remember. Have a look at the **BNF Cook's Club** for healthy eating recipes and to learn new skills. Useful if you do Food Technology too.

www.fdf.org.uk
Try the Food and Drink Federation.

The quiz was helpful.

www.schoolscience.co.uk

Click on **The Heart And Circulation**.

There are six sections to click on and find out information about the heart and circulation. Some of the facts are really interesting. The diagrams are good too.

You only need to know about circulation in the context of transporting products of digestion. So don't get too bogged down in learning the heart's structure, as you won't be tested on it in KS3. Try the quiz at the end.

www.bhf.org.uk
The British Heart Foundation.

You can hear a heart rate monitor beeping while you are on the main page and it gets really annoying. I couldn't work out how to make it stop.

www.learn.co.uk

Click on **Enter learn.co.uk Here** then **Key Stage 3 Science**. Look down the *Life Processes and Living Things* list and click on **Human Respiration** followed by **All Life Processes Need Energy**.

Try the true/false quiz at the start. Make sure you read the summary at the end, which is good for revision.

Don't confuse breathing and respiration – they are different processes. You should know the word equation for respiration.

www.sambal.co.uk/respiration.html

www.sciencenet.org.uk/database/bio/biosublist.html

Click on **Microbiology**, then **Is It True That There Are About A Million Germs On Every Pinhead?**.

There are some good facts about microbes here. The Level 1 answers are easy to understand for the average pupil in Year 8; Level 2 and 3 answers get more challenging.

There are lots of other questions and answers to take a look at, so go back to the **Microbiology** home page and select some of the others. You should know that microbes can either cause harm or do us good. Know an example for each.

people.ku.edu/%7Ejbrown/bugs.html
Bugs in the news!

www.who.int/en/
Try the World Health Organisation

www.amnh.org/nationalcenter/infection/02_bac/02_bac.html
Look at bacteria in the cafeteria and try the games, too.

www.howstuffworks.com/immune-system.htm

Go through all the main topics, like **Seeing Your Immune System** or **Basics of the Immune System**.

The **Using All Of This New Knowledge** section has lots of information about how vaccinations work.

You need to know how vaccinations work, and you should know the ways your body keeps microbes out, for example acid in your stomach, or mucus in your windpipe.

whyfiles.org/coolimages/archives.html?cat=4
Want to see what the flu virus looks like? Click on **Health**, then scroll down to the influenza virus electron photo micrograph. Click on it for a larger image and more information.

www.bbc.co.uk/health/immune/
More information on the immune system.

Lots of information and pictures on all the body systems but not a lot to do, like games or quizzes.

www.healthfinder.gov/kids/

Click on **Cool And Uncool Stuff**, choose from **Alcohol**, **Drugs**, **Exercise** or **Smoking**, then follow the links.

There are some great games on this website. Make sure you try the quiz on alcohol.

Have a look at all four areas, alcohol, drugs, exercise and smoking, as you need to know how all four affect the body.

kidshealth.org/kid/stay_healthy/body/smoking.html

www.purchon.com/health/dangers.htm

www.dnaftb.org/dnaftb/1/concept/

Explore the links, starting with **Children Resemble Their Parents**. There are 41 classic genetic topics to choose from. Pick out the ones that interest you.

Try 1–10 first. See how you get on, as some of the later topics move towards GCSE standard or further. For each topic you look at, make sure you click on **Problem** to check what you've learnt. The animations are worth clicking on too.

Best suited to Levels 5–7 pupils. Don't forget: if you are interested in genetics, get your school to support 'jeans for genes' day every Autumn. The money raised goes towards genetic research. Make sure you know where genes are in the cell.

www.bbc.co.uk/genes/
More information on genetics.

Hard.

www.aboutdarwin.com

This website is dedicated to the life and times of Charles Darwin, a famous biologist you will definitely learn about in KS3.

Teachers love setting research homework on this scientist, so use this website to help. It has everything you could possibly want to find out about Charles Darwin. He was recently voted in the top 10 of the 100 greatest Britons.

www.galapagos.org/gallery.html
Beautiful photographs of the Galapagos Islands.

www.darwinfoundation.org/Restoring/index.html
See the famous Galapagos tortoises.

www.strangescience.net/darwin.htm and school.discovery.com/schooladventures/galapagos/
More information on Darwin.

I'd never heard of the Galapagos Islands. The giant tortoises look sweet.

www.roslin.ac.uk

Click **Public Interest**, then **Cloning**.

A fascinating website about how Dolly the sheep was created and the ethical problems associated with cloning.

Have a look at **Discussion Papers And Press Articles** for lots of links on cloning. Also have a look at the **Image Library**. Make sure you understand the basic process of cloning.

www.geneletter.com/archives/twentyonearguments.html
This factual site offers the arguements for and against cloning.

www.bbc.co.uk/genes
More information about cloning.

Wierd stuff, like cloning your pet.

www.museums.org.za/sam/quagga/quagga.htm

Click on **Extinction Is Forever** and read through. Then go to **Why The Quagga Became Extinct** and **The Aim Of The Project**.

This website is about an amazing project, which aims to recreate the extinct quagga (a variety of zebra), using DNA technology and selective breeding. Have a look at the **Frequently Asked Questions**. There are some lovely pictures of quaggas on this website, which show you what this unusual animal looked like.

There was a question about the quagga on the 2003 SATs/NC tests, so this site is worth a look. Make sure you know the difference between selective breeding and natural selection.

www.oneworld.net/penguin/
Tiki the penguin presents his site on endangered species and extinction.

What an unusual animal. I thought this was a joke.

www.sciencenet.org.uk/database/bio/biosublist.html

Click on **Photosynthesis**, then **What Is Photosynthesis And Why Is It Important?**.

A good website with lots of information about plants and photosynthesis. Make sure you look at all the *Level 2* questions and answers. These can all be accessed from the main **Photosynthesis** home page.

Make sure you know the word equation for photosynthesis. The *Level 3* questions and answers get quite detailed and are really GCSE standard, but if you are working at National Curriculum Level 6+ then you should take a look anyway.

www.alienexplorer.com/ecology/topic3.html
More information on photosynthesis.

www.funology.com/laboratory/lab051.cfm
Try some experiments at home on photosynthesis.

www.sciencemadesimple.com

Click on **Science Subjects**, then **Why Do Leaves Change Colour In The Fall?**.

Great information here about photosynthesis. The main section gives clear, detailed answers to the title question. **I Can Read** pages are written in clear language, probably best for Levels 3–6 pupils. **Learn More About It** pages are more difficult and have more detail. These pages would probably be good for Levels 6 and 7 pupils.

Know the word equation for photosynthesis. Read the fun facts and have a go at the word scramble. There are also some good projects to try at home.

www.alienexplorer.com/ecology/topic3.html
More information on photosynthesis.

www.esf.edu/pubprog/brochure/leaves/leaves.htm
More on why leaves change colour in Autumn.

www.sciencenet.org.uk/database/bio/biosublist.html

Click on **Cell Biology**, then **What Is A Cell?**.

There is lots of good, easily understood information about cells here. However there are no diagrams, which is a shame.

There are three levels to click on. Work through Level 1 and then try Level 2, which uses more of the scientific words you need to know, like cytoplasm, cell membrane and nucleus. Have a look at some of the other sections on this website, as it's full of fascinating questions and answers about science in general.

www.eurekascience.com/ICanDoThat/
Click on any of the cells in the list for information on plant, animal and bacterial cells.

www.pbs.org/wgbh/aso/databank/index.html

This takes you to the home page of the *People and Discoveries* site. Click on **People** to go straight to a list of famous scientists and what they are famous for. Choose one, click on the link and all the information and photos are there.

Make sure you click on each of the main topics on the home page, such as **Medicine And Health**. You can then see a list of famous scientists in this category, which you can click on for more information. Best of all on these pages, you get a list of dates and discoveries in that area. Some are fascinating. Click on one that interests you. The **Related Features** at the end are really fun.

oak.cc.conncoll.edu/~mzim/dead.html
The *Great Chemists Who Aren't Dead White* Guys site.

Wow! I loved this website! Useful for homework.

www.astr.ua.edu/4000WS/4000WS.html

Scroll down the home page to see what the website is all about and then click on **Introduction**.

This website is called *4000 Years of Women in Science* and it's all about famous female scientists and what they have done. These ladies had original 'girl power'. Take a look via the main **Biography** section and impress your teachers. There are photos too.

Try the **Interactive Quiz** on the history of women in science. You can also put your name in the site's **Hall of Fame**.

www.factmonster.com/spot/whmbios2.html
Another good source of biographies. The science pages here are good too.

I now have lots of information about how us women have contributed to science to annoy the boys in my science class with. I never knew there were so many.

www.forestry.gov.uk

Click on **Wild Woods** then scroll right down to the bottom. Choose a habitat to look at from the list by clicking on it.

Practise your classification of animals while at this site by clicking on one of the taxonomic groups to see some good photographs and examples of animals in British woodlands.

Use the website's search facility to find woodlands where you might see some of the animals you have read about. Then ask an adult or even your school to take you there for some fieldwork! You should know the five taxonomic groups for animals and examples for each.

www.ucmp.berkeley.edu/help/taxaform.html

www.hhmi.org/coolscience/critters/critters.html
More on taxonomy.

I never knew Britain had poisonous snakes in its woodlands!

www.science.howstuffworks.com/animal-camouflage.htm

This web address takes you straight to where you need to be.

As you click through the pages there is lots of information about how animals are adapted to their environments. There are lovely, clear photographs of different organisms. In particular, there is an excellent picture of the arctic fox showing how it adapts to seasonal changes.

At the end of the camouflage information, there is a **Lots More Information** section. Have a look at **How Do Zebras' Stripes Act As Camouflage?** and **Why Do Chameleons Change Colour?**. You should know examples of how organisms are adapted to their environments.

The artic fox is so cute. It's amazing how it changes colour.

www.harcourtschool.com/activity/camouflage/camouflage.html

This web address takes you straight to the correct page.

A lovely, interactive website. You click on an environment for a hidden animal search. You get given a choice of animals and have to choose which one is best adapted to that environment. It's a fun game.

This teaches the idea of camouflage and adaptation well. Try all the habitats. It's quite easy and best suited for Levels 2–4 pupils.

I enjoyed this even though it was easy for me. It was nice getting it all right for a change.

www.nationalgeographic.com

Click on **For Kids**, then **NG Explorer** **Classroom Magazine**, then **Online Adventures**. Click on **Great Barrier Reef** and **Start Adventure**. Read the information about the habitat of the Great Barrier Reef in Australia then click **Dive Now**. Click on any of the organisms on the underwater scene for more information.

After you have found out about the reef creatures, go to **Scavenger Hunt** to check what you have learnt.

Make sure you understand what a habitat is and that you know other examples of habitats. Try to work out how these creatures are adapted to live in the Great Barrier Reef.

If you are interested in marine conservation try. www.gbrmpa.gov.au

Cool.

Interdependence

How to use it

Look out for

Hints

Other links

Student comments

www.sciencemadesimple.com

Click on **Science Made Simple**, then **How Do Animals Spend the Winter?**.

The main section gives clear detailed answers to the title question. **I Can Read** pages are written in clear language, probably best for Levels 3–6 pupils. **Learn More About It** pages are more difficult and have more detail. These are best for Levels 6 and 7 pupils.

Make sure you know a couple of examples of how animals survive the winter, then have a go at some of the fun projects. For example, there is a recipe for bird food for the winter. You can also subscribe to a newsletter, which answers all sorts of other science questions like 'Why is ice slippery?'.

Have a look at the arctic fox as an example of one organism's way to survive the winter. This often comes up in exam questions. www.science.howstuffworks.com/animal-camouflage.htm

www.uksafari.com

Click on **Plants And Trees**. You then have five taxonomic plant groups to choose from.

Have a look at all the taxonomic groups: fungi, lichens, ferns, flowering plants, trees. There are great photographs for each group and lots of interesting facts.

You should know the main taxonomic groups of plants and be able to describe some common features.

www.nhm.ac.uk/hosted_sites/bps/
Good pictures of ferns.

You can download free wallpaper and make greetings cards showing different organisms from different taxonomic groups. Some weird plants!

www.gould.edu.au/foodwebs/kids_web.htm

Choose a habitat for which you want to build a food web. You then get a host of organisms and a blank food web to place them in. All the instructions are on the page.

If you get an organism wrong you must reselect it and try putting it in another group. There are lots of clues to help if you don't know the organism or what it eats.

This is good practice for using the rules for building food webs, and tests knowledge of words like omnivore, herbivore and carnivore which you need to know. You can print out your finished food web.

I really enjoyed this!

www.bishops.ntc.nf.ca/science/biology/EnergyFlow/sld001.htm

This web address takes you to the start of a slide show.

Click the play button to go through each slide. The 17 slides cover facts on energy flow through ecosystems, food chains and webs, as well as pyramids of numbers and biomass.

Click on the **A** button and you get a clear definition of the key words and titles from the slide you are on. Learn these.

Simple layout with clear information. The pictures are a bit rubbish, as they are too small to see, but the facts make it worth a visit.

Interdependence

How to use it

Look out for

Hints

Other links

Student comments

www.alienexplorer.com/ecology/topic4.html

Click through all the topics under the *Food Chains* title.

There are good definitions and examples of food chains and webs. Read through all the sections.

Have a look at the pond food web. What would happen if all the trout died? You need to be able to work out the effect on other organisms in the food chain if one organism is removed. Remember, the arrow always points to the eater and all food chains start with a green plant.

www.epa.gov/pesticides

Click on **About Pesticides** then click on any of the seven questions.

Remember, using pesticides can maximise food production but many other useful organisms are killed in the process. You should know the example of DDT, a pesticide that caused problems to animals at the top of food chains. It is now banned in many countries.

To find out why DDT is such a persistent pesticide go to:
www.epa.gov/pbt/ddt.htm

www.chem.ox.ac.uk/mom/ddt/ddt.html

wwwpersonal.umich.edu/~nlacros/pollution.html

A bit boring. No animation or games. The information was a bit worrying though.

www.newscientist.com

Scroll down to the *Hot Topics* heading and click on **Pollution**, then click on **Quizzes** and **Is One Planet Enough?**.

There are quite a lot of questions in this quiz – so there's a lot of reading – but they are all quite easy questions about your lifestyle.

You need to know that the way we live has a big impact on our planet and that because of this our environment is changing. After taking the test, make a list of things you can do to be more environmentally friendly. Then aim to do one of these things for 1 month.

www.darvill.clara.net/hotpots/SpaceshipEarth.htm
Another quiz on environmental issues.

I was horrified to find out that if everyone lived like me we'd need three extra planets to support us! I thought I wasn't too bad to the environment. I'm going to ask my mum to start recycling stuff more.

www.newscientist.com

Scroll down to the *Hot Topics* section and click on **Population** then **Quizzes**.

This online quiz tests how environmentally conscious you are in your everyday life. Each question is about the choices you make daily and the effects these have on the planet. After you have got your score, go back and click on **Answers** so you can see how each choice is affecting the environment.

If you score badly, think about why your choices are damaging the environment and what alternatives would be better for the planet's future. The **Answers** section will help with this.

There's so much to read about on this website. Some was too hard for me, but some Level 7 pupils might find it easier.

library.thinkquest.org/11226/index.htm

Click on **Click Here** to proceed to the *Chemical Carousel.*

Read the first page then click on the forward arrow. You will find out about Captain Carbon's trip around the carbon cycle.

You need to know that the materials that make up organisms are recycled. The carbon cycle is a good example. The basis of the carbon cycle is that photosynthesis removes carbon from the cycle while respiration, burning and rotting add carbon to the atmosphere.

www.chem4kids.com/files/elements/006_speak.html
Find out more about carbon and its importance for life.

www.epa.gov/globalwarming/kids/index.html
Find out how mankind's disturbance of the carbon cycle is leading to global warming/the greenhouse effect.

library.thinkquest.org/11922/

Click on any of the animal groups in the zoo: **Bears**, **Monkey Island**, **Panda Paradise** and **Extinct Animals** are just some of the options.

At the bottom of the page click on **Habitats**. This is the more informative part of the site. Click on the graph or links to find out more about each habitat and the animals living there.

You need to know that habitats are changing due to many factors, e.g. humans destroying them. So keep an eye out for any information on this.

www.uen.org/themepark/html/habitat/endhab.html

This address takes you to the correct page.

Take a look at the virtual tour of a **Rainforest**. Visit endangered Africa and take the **Congo Virtual Tour**. These are both really interesting habitats. Use this site to find out why some animals are endangered and which ones. There is also good information on how animals are adapted to their environments.

You need to know reasons why habitats are changing, and that if organisms don't change and adapt with the environment they will die.

www.greenpeace.org
Greenpeace has a good website with lots of information about endangered species and habitats.

www.sandiegozoo.org
Also try San Diego zoo.

The virtual tours are fun.

www.wpbschoolhouse.btinternet.co.uk

Scroll right down and click on the green panel called **Quizzes For KS3**. Then click on **Twf** or **Tmc** in the *7G* row.

This is either a word-fill exercise (wf) or multiple-choice questions (mc) to complete. The content is all needed for KS3 science and is very good for checking your understanding of key words relating to states of matter and *how* things are arranged in them.

Make sure that you remember how particles move in solids, liquids and gases. This is needed for all levels in SATs.

www.darvill.clara.net
Go to **Site Map**, scroll down to **Particles**, click on **Particle Worksheet** and try to complete it. Download and keep for revision.

It was easy to read but some of the words are hard to remember. I liked the word-fill.

www.science-active.co.uk

Click on **Key Stage 3**, then **Getting Hot – Changing State**.

This page is lesson 2 from a series on this site. The use of colours is good and so are the ideas for testing your understanding of the words used when we heat solids, liquids and gases. Make sure that you follow what is happening to the water as it changes state.

There is an excellent paragraph explaining that we should look at how much water or ice is being used. This idea of *how much* is so important in Chemistry.

I like the way it is set out. I could name things by using the mouse and moving the words.

www.bbc.co.uk/schools/ks3bitesize/science/

Click on **Chemistry**, then **Classifying Materials 1 Revise** and move to **Page 1**.

You will find a table with lots of ways to describe a solid, a liquid and a gas. You need to know that solids and liquids are not easily compressed – that means squashed – to fit in a smaller space.

Try to learn the words that are on the screen – sometimes you have to fill in a table a bit like this one in your SATs.

www.learn.co.uk
Follow the links to the KS3 science pages on **Properties Of Solids, Liquids And Gases**. Use the **Kinetic Theory Of Matter** page as well. These have good words and meanings to learn.

Easy peasy!

www.sep.org.uk

Click on the small **Curriculum Resources** link, then **Diffusion In A Gel** and **Detailed Notes**. Wait for the note to download.

This page has a method to show that colour moves through a gel by diffusion. 'Diffusion' is a key word for KS3 and into GCSE as well. Read the method in the box and see if you can follow what the class did.

Diffusion happens in solids, liquids and gases and you should try to remember an example of each.

www.learn.co.uk
Follow the links to the KS3 science pages on **Kinetic Theory Of Matter**.

It was a lot of reading but the method looks like fun. My teacher says we can try it out.

www.rudimentsofwisdom.com

Welcome to the *Rudiments of Wisdom Cartoon Encylopaedia!* Click on **Science** and **Pressure**.

This page is a cartoon strip that explains the history of pressure in gases. It tells the story of discoveries to do with gases. Read it and possibly make bullet points about the gases that you have read about.

Try to remember the units that are used to measure the pressure in a gas. Remember the objects that use gas pressures, like tyres.

www.learn.co.uk
Follow the links to the KS3 science pages, scroll down and click on **Elements, Compounds and Mixtures** and **Changes Of State, Gas Pressure And Diffusion**.

The cartoons have lots of facts and are fun and different to read.

www.e-gfl.org

Work through the following sequence of links: **Secondary Pupils**, **KS3**, **Learning Zone**, **Science** and **Changing Matter Notes**.

The first page has pupil and teacher notes. Scroll down to the purple boxes, **Activity** or **Worksheet** – you should try both. These are animated sequences that really show particles vibrating faster when heated and so explain why they can change state.

There are very important facts on both these pages, so spend some time here to learn the words and pictures that you can use to explain them.

www.bbc.co.uk/schools/ks3bitesize/science/
Find the pages on **Chemistry**, click on **Changing Materials** and work through the revision for **Physical Changes**.

We liked this a lot. The pictures really helped us to see what melting and boiling look like.

www.bbc.co.uk/schools/KS3bitesize/science/chemistry

Click on **Changing Materials 2** and **Geological Changes**. Work through the pages for **Revise** and the **Test**.

These pages have some really good pictures of rocks that you are expected to know for KS3. Look for grains, layers and colours. Think about rates of cooling.

You are trying to understand that the longer the cooling period, the larger the crystals.

www.learn.co.uk
Follow the links to KS3 science and click on **Geological Changes**. Work through the bullet points on the left-hand side of the screen.

I found this easy to do and the photos were clear.

www.usgs.gov

Click on **Students And Teachers** then **Rocks And Images** on the right-hand side.

This is the US Geological Survey's site. It has a general description of how different rocks are formed. At the bottom of the text there are three icons: igneous, sedimentary and metamorphic. Click on any one of these!

Make some notes and learn some rock names. Go back and choose another subject, e.g. volcanoes. You can get up-to-date and almost up-to-the minute information about the volcanic activity on Hawaii! Click on **Real-Time Info**.

www.scishop.org
Select **The Rock Cycle** and click **Go**. Work through the options for this learning objective. This is all good revision for SATs and GCSE.

The volcano stuff is brilliant!

www.exploratorium.edu

Click on **Try This**, then on **Salt Volcano** from the *Planet Earth* list.

A hands-on activity here for making a lava lamp, but always ask permission before you start.

The method is simple and shows how different things behave when mixed together. Try to remember some Year 7 words to describe what is happening here.

www.usgs.gov
Type in 'Hawaiian Volcano Observatory' and click on **Volcano Watch** on the left-hand menu. Finally, click on **Kilauea**. Scroll through this page and click on the pictures to see up-to-date images of real volcanoes erupting.

Worked fine.

www.darvill.clara.net

Click on Site Map, scroll down and click on the Elements, Mixtures and Compounds Quiz.

This is a colourful site which allows you to choose your answers and get them checked. You should really make sure you are clear about the differences between elements and compounds from the pictures here.

There are mixtures here also, so make sure you understand the differences between these and elements and compounds – such a lot of words to remember!

www.bbc.co.uk/schools/ks3bitesize/science/
Click on Chemistry, click on Classifying Materials 1, and work through the Test and Revise sections.

Very easy and I really could see the different types.

www.karentimberlake.com

Click on **Chemodules**, then **Atoms And Elements**.

These are downloadable *PowerPoint* presentations. Use the small icon at the bottom left-hand corner and click on it when you want to move onto the next slide. Left-click your mouse to get the add-ins on the screen. Try to answer the questions as they appear. This is a good site and the slides are clear and accurate.

Try to learn some of the names as you go through this site – it leads well into GCSE. This content is at Levels 5–7 and is well worth working at.

www.learn.co.uk
Find the KS3 science section, scroll down and click on **Elements, Compounds and Mixtures**. Click on **Elements** and then **Compounds** at the left-hand side. Work through the objectives.

Clear but hard!

www.webelements.com

Click on one of the elements and you get key information about that element.

The elements are arranged in the Periodic Table. There are only this number of elements known, which means that the total number of boxes here is the total number of elements that we know of. Try clicking on **O** for oxygen and see the information that you get back – it is an awesome site with loads of good info.

Try looking up the elements that you have never heard of before.

www.kids.net.au
Click on **Schooltime Science**, **Chemistry**, **Chemistry Functions**, and finally **Periodic Table**.

I spent ages looking up really funny-sounding ones.

www.chem4kids.com

Click on **Elements**.

The page that comes up has a Periodic Table and in-depth information about the first 18 elements.

Look up each of the elements and see how much you can learn.

www.funbrain.com/periodic

Helped to get my head around the names and the whole table thing.

www.learn.co.uk

Click on **Enter learn.co.uk Here**, then **Key Stage 3 Science**. Scroll down to *Materials and their Properties* and click on **Elements**.

What do we think is inside the atom? Spend a little time looking at this section.

Use the other topics on the left-hand side to help you see that an element has only one type of atom. Make sure you understand and remember this fact.

www.wpbschoolhouse.btinternet.co.uk
Select **KS3**, find the *8E* section and explore.

www.scishop.org

Select **Compounds And Elements** from the drop-down menu, select **How Are Elements And Compounds Different** from the next menu, then click **Search**. Click on the www.ultranet.com page listed.

This is a useful site and it uses the correct terms to describe atoms, elements and compounds. It explains the methods of separating mixtures, so make sure that you read it carefully and remember what you have done in class.

Key separation methods are chromatography, distillation and filtration.

www.saburchill.com
Click on **Chemistry**, type in 'elements and compounds', click on **Find It** and click on **Chemical Names** to find a good page to study.

www.brainpop.com

Click on **Science**, then **Compounds And Mixtures**.

Play the quiz first of all and then watch the movie – don't forget the sound! This is a helpful movie if you need to practise the words associated with elements, mixtures and compounds.

Make a note of the mixtures that they give you: soda, shaving foam and a few others. These are often put as questions in SATs.

www.bbc.co.uk/schools/ks3bitesize/science/
Click on **Chemistry**, **Classifying Materials 1**, and choose the **Revise** option and then the **Test**. All the information here is SATs stuff.

The movie helps you to see mixtures better.

www.wpbschoolhouse.btinternet.co.uk

Select **KS3** from the drop-down menu, scroll down to *8E* and click on **Twf**, the word-fill, or **Tmc** for the multiple-choice questions.

The Twf and Tmc get harder. Download and get them 'word perfect'.

This idea of atoms in combinations and equations is for Levels 4–7 and so it is important that you spend some time trying to learn some simple ones at least.

www.learn.co.uk
Click on **Enter learn.co.uk Here** and **Key Stage 3 Science**, scroll down and click on **Elements, Compounds and Mixtures**. Click on **More Chemical Reactions** and work through the equations. You should get as much practice on these as possible.

The word-fills are good practice. I did them till I got them right.

www.bbc.co.uk/schools/ks3bitesize/science

Click on **Chemistry**, then **Chemical Reactions** **Revise**.

All the pages here are very good for explaining what a chemical reaction is and how scientists show that a chemical reaction has taken place by writing a chemical equation. An equation is just another way of showing how particles arrange and rearrange themselves in a chemical reaction.

This is all really good preparation for GCSE. Equations and reactions come up all the time and if you really try now then it will help in KS4.

www.wpbschoolhouse.btinternet.co.uk
Select **KS3** from the drop-down menu and click the options in rows *9E* and *9F*. Both the word-fill and the multi-choice questions are really good because these are all SATs-style questions.

I did need some help with this and I thought this site was brill.

www.learn.co.uk

Click on **Enter learn.co.uk Here**, then **Key Stage 3 Science**. Scroll down and click on **Chemical Changes**, **Energy Changes In Reactions** and **Exothermic Or Endothermic Reactions**.

It is important to know the difference between 'endothermic' and 'exothermic'. The main idea here is *energy*.

Remember the equipment that is used in a reaction and how to use it safely. Remember that a thermometer measures temperature and you would need one for this type of experiment. Use the other topic buttons to find out more.

www.sciencenet.org.uk
Click on **Chemistry**, **Q+As** and **Structure And Bonding**. Scroll down to the questions that include 'endothermic' and 'exothermic'.

Good pictures, but still hard.

science.howstuffworks.com

Click on **Physical Science** and **How C-4 Works**.

This site tells you about burning and combustion. This is a type of chemical reaction that gives out tremendous energy.

Remember your exothermic reactions.

www.learn.co.uk
Hit **Enter learn.co.uk Here**, **Key Stage 3** **Science**, then scroll down and click on **Chemical Changes**. Click on **Combustion** on the left-hand side of the screen. Download this helpful page.

Cool!

www.wpbschoolhouse.btinternet.co.uk

Select **KS3** from the drop-down menu and scroll down. Work through the notes pages, then do the quizzes, **Twf** and **Tmc**.

These pages and quizzes are all good for SATs and go right up to Level 7. You should make sure that you are familiar with chemical reactions and the *types* of reactions that elements and compounds undergo.

For all the reactions, you could try to learn the equations that go with them. In addition, the energy changes that go with reactions are very often questioned on Level 6+ at SATs.

www.sciencenet.org.uk
Click on **Chemistry**, **Q+As** and **Structure And Bonding**. Make sure you are familiar with types of reactions.

The Schoolhouse quizzes are hard but I feel more confident about reactions now.

www.wpbschoolhouse.btinternet.co.uk

Select **KS3** from the drop-down menu, click on the quiz options in row *9F* and work your way in particular through to 9F/3 and 9F/4.

Find the word-fills and quizzes that test your ability to rearrange atoms in chemical equations. This site is really helpful because you can check your answers and also download the worksheets.

Use the **Tmp** matching pairs game to help with names and formulae of compounds in reactions.

You have to know quite a bit before you can do these, but they are good and really help.

www.karentimberlake.com

Click on **Chemodules**, **Chemical Reactions And Quantities** and finally **Chemical Equations**.

This is a downloadable *PowerPoint* presentation and is *excellent*! Use the forward and backward buttons on the keyboard to navigate around the file. Go up to slide 17 and really make use of the material. Have a pen and paper handy to practise the equations and make a very clear note of the idea that mass must total in an equation.

If you were unsure about physical and chemical changes, then the first few slides will really help. Using this *PowerPoint* presentation will also improve your ICT skills. This work is really at Levels 6 upwards.

www.sciencenet.org.uk
Click on **Chemistry**, **Q+As** and **Materials**, then scroll through the formulae questions.

I am in Year 8 and I got the ideas OK!

www.karentimberlake.com

Click on **Chemodules**, click on **Types Of Chemical Reaction** and wait for the *PowerPoint* show to download.

The first 10 slides are good at showing you some equations. They are quite hard but the ideas of rearrangement are good.

Write some down to test yourself on later.

www.bbc.co.uk/schools/ks3bitesize/science
Click on **Chemistry**, **Chemical Reactions** and work through the **Revise** section and then the **Test**. Make sure you get these right!

Hard, but I like the *PowerPoint* because the answers appear from nowhere!

www.science.demon.co.uk

Welcome to *Dr M's Science Site*. Click on **Science Homework**, click on **Chemical Changes** and up comes the worksheet.

This has questions that you need for Year 8 Chemistry as well as for Year 9 simple equations. Complete it and print it off. You should get the correct answers to help with revision for SATs.

Use the advice and move the mouse over the test tubes to get an idea of the chemical reactions.

www.wpbschoolhouse.btinternet.co.uk
Select **KS3**, then find the *9H* row and click **Twf**. Check your answers well! There is a lot to take in here.

A bit hard but makes you try.

www.saburchill.com

Click on **Chemistry**, type in **Rules For Chemical Reactions**, click **Find It!**. Scroll down the results of the search and click on the site labelled **Equations Using Symbols and Formulae**.

This is a fab page! It takes you through how to use symbols and how to write and balance equations. The introduction is very important because it tells you that you can't lose or make atoms. In other words, you must balance up the numbers of atoms before and after the reaction. Atoms have mass so you must balance your masses too!

Using the Periodic Table, look at masses and try to put them into the equations. You'll soon see that an equation must balance by mass.

www.wpbschoolhouse.btinternet.co.uk
Select **KS3** then click on **Tmc** at the very bottom of the page. This is a test which covers all years of KS3.

www.bgfl.org

Click on Pupils 11–16, then on KS3, Learning Zone, Science, Acids And Alkalis Start. Finally, choose Litmus Reactions and work through the pages.

This is a colourful site and asks you questions.

Print off your tests/answers and get your teacher to check your work.

www.learn.co.uk
Click on Enter learn.co.uk Here and Key Stage 3 Science, then scroll down and click on Acids And Alkalis. Click on the objectives on the left-hand side of the screen. These are all needed for GCSE as well. Good luck!

It was pretty, but we fell out trying to do it.

www.scishop.org

Select **Using Chemistry** from the drop-down menu, then **What Types Of New Materials Are Made?** and click **Search**. Click on **Million.doc** when the search is complete and download the *Word* file.

This is a great test of your knowledge! There are questions here that cover all aspects of chemical reactions from simple formulae to mass balances! The work is at about Level 5+ but there are some higher level questions here too.

Make sure you get the correct answers – this page will also help with GCSE work.

www.wpbschoolhouse.btinternet.co.uk
Find the *9H* section after selecting **KS3** from the drop-down menu.

Long, but makes you think.

www.wpbschoolhouse.btinternet.co.uk

Select **KS3** from the drop-down menu, find section *9E* and click on **Twf** for the word-fill or **Tmc** for the multiple-choice tests.

The word-fill uses the terms that you will need in order to describe reactions of metals with acids, oxygen and water. This really will help to raise your Level up to 6+ if you go through all the word-fills and tests. There is also a longer test which will require you to recall not just the metals but also other parts of Chemistry. Have a go – you might surprise yourself!

As the quizzes get harder you've got to think more.

www.chem4kids.com

Click on **Reactions** and **Acids And Bases**.

The first page to scroll down and read deals with some everyday examples of acids and bases. After that comes the real Chemistry, which may look a bit difficult, but just try it. There are bits here which are Levels 6–7 but have a go!

Remember your pH scale here and the uses of indicators.

www.topmarks.co.uk
Search for 'chemical reactions'.

www.spartechsoftware.com/reeko

This is *Reeko's Mad Sci Lab*. Scroll down, find the heading *Chemical Reaction in Action*, and click on **This Experiment**.

This is an experiment between steel wool and vinegar. You need to remember your reactivity of metals series to understand it.

This is Levels 5+ work and the reactivity series is examined every year without fail!

www.wpbschoolhouse.btinternet.co.uk
Select **KS3** and then click **Tmc** at the bottom of the page for the 20-question test.

A bit smelly!

www.lowtonhs.net

Click **Revision**, then **Science Revision** and **Metals**.

Scroll down to the first two questions and answers. This is all very good stuff to read and try to remember. It is Levels 6+ and into GCSE-level but the reactions of the metals are the same in both KS3 and KS4.

Have a copy of the reactivity series of metals close by when you are reading this page.

www.learn.co.uk
Click on **Enter learn.co.uk Here** and **Key Stage 3 Science**, then scroll down and click on anything under the heading *Materials and their Properties*. Choose any of the objectives because they all take you through KS3.

Good bullet points to copy and learn.

www.learn.co.uk

Click on **Enter learn.co.uk Here**, choose **Key Stage 3 Science** then **Forces And Motion** from the *Physical Processes* menu.

Once again learn.co.uk has the answers! These pages deal with balanced and unbalanced forces, moments, the pressure equation, friction and air resistance.

Click on the red words to see their definitions. The summary and glossary are very useful.

This website links very well with the forces pages of www.zephyrus.co.uk.

www.exploratorium.edu/skateboarding

Click **Trick Science** to look at the science and forces behind skateboarding tricks. Navigate by clicking **Backside** and **Frontside**.

How do you 'ollie'? How do skaters go so high in a half-pipe? A website dedicated to the science behind skateboarding – how cool!

Click the **Activity** icon to find activities and experiments to show how the forces behind skateboarding work.

www.zephyrus.co.uk
This site has a good section on forces.

Real-life examples of forces. Quite complicated science though.

www.eoascientific.com/interactive

Everything you need to know about mass, weight, volume and density. Click on the **Space** icon and then **Density**.

Fully interactive, with movies and computer demos.

Doing the experiment with the sound on is really cool. The voice tells you exactly what to do! Remember to record your results as you go.

Takes a long time to load up.

www.zephyrus.co.uk

Choose the **Magnetism** option from the Physics menu on the left-hand side of the screen. Click the **More** icon to scroll through the screens.

Try making the electromagnet. You may need an adult to help you with this.

Test your knowledge by clicking on the **Activities** icon and choosing the **Magnetism** activities.

Gives the facts in a good way, with pictures to help.

www.schoolscience.co.uk

Hold your cursor over the **Resources** icon and select **Physics** then **11–14** from the menu. From the next menu, choose **Electromagnets**.

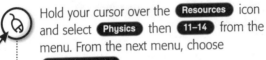

Scroll over the blue text and watch the diagrams. Test your knowledge in the quizzes at the bottom of every page.

You need to know how to make electromagnets stronger for your SATs.

Gives good examples, such as the electric bell.

www.enter.net/~dlandis/main.htm

This address takes you straight to where you need to be.

There are a lot of complicated (university level!) pages on aerodynamics on the web – this is the best for you. The core of the information on this web page could easily be in your SATs.

Take a few notes.

www.exploratorium.edu/cycling/index.html
The aerodynamics site eventually links to this cycling site, which makes interesting reading.

www.fi.edu/qa97/spotlight3

This address takes you straight to the page you need. Follow the links for **Extra Information**.

A web page that shows simple machines, e.g. levers. Follow the links to fantastic pages on Leonardo da Vinci.

www.keveney.com/Engines.html
Animations of more advanced machines.

www.schoolscience.co.uk

Move the cursor over the **Resources** icon, select **Physics**, then click the **11–14** option. Choose **Aerosols And Pressure** from the menu.

The main areas of interest are **Pressure** and **How Do Gases Behave?** for pressure within gases.

Click red words to get definitions and watch the animations as you move the cursor over the blue words. You will need to refresh the page to see the animations again.

Very easy to understand.

brp.arc.nasa.gov

Click the **Enter** icon and select **Science** from the menu. Choose **Why Gravitational Biology** then **Gravity Basics**.

The rest of this NASA site makes interesting (but heavy-going) reading about a specialised branch of science. The section on gravitational basics contains everything you need to know about gravity.

The information is at a fairly high level so make notes of the key points.

www.zephyrus.co.uk
The forces section of this site has simpler information on gravity.

Quite complicated language.

www.learn.co.uk

Click on **Enter learn.co.uk Here**, choose **Key Stage 3 Science**, then **The Earth And Beyond** from the *Physical Processes* menu.

Whilst this is a comprehensive website on the Solar System, it is the page on **Satellites** that is of most interest here.

Do the **Prior Knowledge** quiz before going through the site.

www.pbs.org/wgbh/nova/barrier

This address takes you straight to the best place.

A seriously action-packed site! Here you'll find the history of attempts to break the sound barrier, plus info on sonic booms and the fastest vehicles on ground, water and in the air.

Good background reading.

This is a very detailed site. There is a lot to read.

www.eoascientific.com/interactive

Click on the **Space** icon and then the **Solar System** icon.

A very detailed website with lots of extra information, for example about asteroid impacts.

This is a fairly tricky website to navigate around but the information it contains is very detailed.

www.seds.org/nineplanets/nineplanets
Another great website on the Solar System.

I found it difficult to find the information.

www.zephyrus.co.uk

Choose the **Solar Systems** option from the Physics menu on the left-hand side of the screen. Click the **More** icon to scroll through the screens.

This web page contains basic, no-nonsense facts about the planets in our Solar System.

You may wish to take a few notes as the Solar Systems topic will definitely be tested in your SATs.

www.nasa.gov
The best website for info on space exploration.

This is much simpler to use than the website listed on page 84 of this book.

www.bbc.co.uk/history/historic_figures/newton_isaac.shtml

This address takes you straight to where you need to be.

There are many websites on the internet dedicated to Sir Isaac Newton, but this is the best one for you! Find out how much Newton's work affects our knowledge and understanding of our world today.

This makes good background reading to several areas of Physics. Take a few notes.

www.zephyrus.co.uk

Choose the **Forces** option from the Physics menu on the left-hand side of the screen. Click the **More** icon to scroll through the screens.

This is a good site that covers many areas of forces, including moments and pressure, balanced and unbalanced forces, upthrust, etc.

This is such a comprehensive website that a few notes are a good idea to help you remember what you have learned.

Has quite a lot of useful information.

edspace.nasa.gov

Use the picture icons to navigate the site.

Could you be an astronaut? How big will the International Space Station be? How do you go to the toilet in space? Find out here.

See if you can click on the fast-moving 'knowtrons' to find bizarre NASA-related facts.

Easy to use but takes a long time to load.

www.brainpop.com

Click **Science**, then choose one of **Fossil Fuels**, **Energy Sources** and **Forms Of Energy**. **Global Warming** is also relevant.

Short, animated science movies. A really good-looking site.

Unless you subscribe you can only use two Brainpop activities per day – choose wisely!

www.zephyrus.co.uk
The energy section will complement these movies.

Annoying that you are limited to two movies a day.

www.eia.doe.gov

Choose **Kid's Page** from the navigation menu.

This website contains lots of information on energy – different types, where we use them, where they come from and their alternatives.

Try the **Energy Quiz** to test your knowledge.

www.green-e.org
This is an example of an attempt at sustainable energy. Lots of very advanced information on pollutants.

www.earthdog.com

Click on **E-Facts**.

The basic facts on solar power, wind power and hydro-electric power are here.

Take a few notes. The **Games** are only good if you understand American Football!

www.azsolarcenter.com
This is the Arizona Solar Centre. Here, they tell you all you need to know about solar power, including the different ways of harnessing solar energy.

A good site.

www.windpower.org

Choose your language (English!) then click on **Wind With Miller**.

Lots of information on wind power – how it works, the parts of a windmill and where a windmill should be sited.

The **Crash Course** is excellent.

A good website. I found it easy to understand.

www.zephyrus.co.uk

Choose the **Energy** option from the Physics menu on the left-hand side of the screen. Click the **More** icon to scroll through the screens.

These pages include the basic information on eight main types of energy.

You need to know these energy types for your SATs.

www.learn.co.uk
Visit the **Energy Resources And Transfer** section for more information.

Gives the information in a quick and easy way.

www.electric-circuits.co.uk

Simply click **Enter** then follow the instructions.

This is a good starting point. The site features basic information on circuits, for example circuit symbols and completing the circuit before a bulb will light. Simple and easy to use.

Aim to get full marks in the quiz!

I knew most of this from primary school. Useful for revision.

www.schoolscience.co.uk/content/3/physics/circuits

Use the page arrow icon at the bottom-left to navigate the site.

Watch the diagrams as you move the cursor over the blue text. Clicking the red text will give you the definition of the word.

Pay attention to where you move the cursor. When certain icons have been activated you have to refresh the whole page to see their action again. Don't forget to try the tests.

www.zephyrus.co.uk

Choose the **Light** option from the Physics menu on the left-hand side of the screen. Click the **More** button to scroll through the screens.

This site contains lots of detailed information on light. Try the shadows activities by clicking the **More** icon. Try extending your knowledge of mirrors and lenses – again by clicking the **More** icon.

Test your knowledge by clicking on the **Activities** icon and choosing the **Light** activities.

Good, real-life examples.

www.zephyrus.co.uk

Choose the **Sound** option from the Physics menu on the left-hand side of the screen. Click the **More** icon to scroll through the screens.

These pages contain only the most basic information on the sound topic.

Sound will definitely come up in your SATs, so take a few notes from these basic pages and then test yourself at the following address.

www.bbc.co.uk/schools/ks3bitesize/science/physics
There's a good test on sound here.

This site has a lot of good, easy-to-understand information on sound.

www.eoascientific.com/interactive

From the menu choose the **Physics And Chemistry** icon, then the **Sound, Light And Radio Waves** icon.

See how changing the frequency, wavelength and amplitude affects the profile of a wave. This is only a single web page, so supplement it by visiting...

gcsephysics.com/pcontent.htm
Choose the **Waves** icon. This is a good, simple GCSE site with additional information on earthquakes and equations (which will not be tested for in your SATs).

www.schoolscience.co.uk

Move the cursor over the **Resources** icon, move down to **Physics** then click the **11–14** option. Choose **Aerosols And Pressure** from the menu.

Most of this information covers pressure, but **Particle Matters** covers changing state.

Clicking on the red words gives definitions, moving the cursor over the blue words activates animations – these have to be reset by refreshing the page.

Easy to find your way around the site.

www.physicscentral.com

Click on **Dear Lou** then **Insulation**.

A wordy web page with no useful diagrams.

Take notes to help you make the most of the information. Insulation could easily come up in a SATs question.

Complex language.

www.learn.co.uk

Click on **Enter learn.co.uk Here**, then go to **Key Stage 3 Science** before choosing **Energy Resources And Transfer**.

An easy-to-follow site with great animations. Deals with conservation of energy, transfer of energy, energy resources and generating electricity.

Read the lesson objectives so you know what to learn from this website.

www.learn.co.uk

I'm sure you know the method by now! Click on **Enter learn.co.uk Here**, choose **Key Stage 3** **Science**, then **Electric Currents And Circuits** from the *Physical Processes* menu.

Once again this is a comprehensive website, but the **Electric Current** web page is particularly good and covers voltage (e.m.f) and amps.

Beware – don't get confused by the 'water pump' model of the flow of electricity.

www.amasci.com/miscon/voltage.html
The information on this web page is very detailed and at a high level.

www.sparkingreaction.info

For the main information on nuclear power click **Find Out More**, then explore the links under the *Database* heading.

An amazing website covering issues such as **What Is Nuclear Power?**, **What Is Radiation?**, **Radiation And Health**, **How Is Radioactive Waste Dealt With?** and **Nuclear Weapons**.

Why not enter the online poll, find tips on reducing your energy consumption and find out how to lobby the government? The games are great!

Interesting. The games are really good.

www.school-for-champions.com

Choose the **Physics** option from the menu, then choose **Heat And Thermodynamics**.

A rather cheesy American website. The information is a bit technical and wordy. Find out what the 'Mpemba effect' is – though it won't be in your SATs! **Heat Transfer**, however, will certainly be in your SATs.

Take notes as you go along to remember the key facts. Do the mini multiple-choice test at the end of each page.

Gives simple-to-understand information.

Student comments

www.nesf.org

Click on the **Home Safety** or **School Safety** icons for some basic information.

The **Home Electrical Safety Quiz** is good.

www.energy.org.uk/EnerSaf-index.htm
In the *General Safety Information* section there are good notes on electricity safety at home and outdoors.

richoq.home.mindspring.com

Simply click the **Megawatts** symbol.

Take the brilliant tour of a powerstation by clicking **Making Megawatts**.

To try the activities, projects and assignments **Click Here**, but beware, several need adult supervision.

Very clear and easy to understand.

www.lignite.com

Choose the **Virtual Tour** from the main menu. Follow the tour by clicking **Begin The Tour** then **Next**.

This site has lots of detailed information on the generation of electricity through burning coal.

Remember that electricity is generated in virtually the same way whether coal, oil or gas is burned.

www.csenergy.com.au
Further info can be found here on the **How Electricity Is Made** page.

A good tour.

www.zephyrus.co.uk

Choose the **Electricity** option from the Physics menu on the left-hand side of the screen. There are three topics to choose from. Work through static electricity, electricity and electrical circuits by clicking the relevant **Enter** icon.

This site contains lots of top-quality information on electricity. The *Dangers of Electricity* page invites you to send your posters on electrical safety to Zephyrus over the internet.

Test your knowledge by clicking on the **Activities** icon in the main Physics menu and choosing the **Electricity** activities.

www.sciencemadesimple.com
Visit the static electricity topic under the **Science Made Simple** icon.

Easy to understand.

www.sciencepages.co.uk

Click on KS3, then choose the year and topic you wish to revise.

A great website that covers loads of topics at KS3. There are quizzes, revision notes, multiple-choice tests and crosswords to try, and lots of links to other useful websites. You can also view pupils' work. Not all topics have resources yet but have a look at the ones that do, like Year 8 food and digestion.

Try as many of the tests and quizzes as you can to check you have understood a topic.

Fantastic!

www.darvill.clara.net/index.htm

Click on **Online Materials**, an icon at the top. Then scroll down the page and choose what you want to revise.

Have a look at the **Revision Tips**. There is information about what sort of learner you are, how to make things stick in your head and how to act in the exams. There are even tips about what equipment to bring.

Knowing what type of learner you are can really help you use the correct revision technique.

The list of ways to revise was helpful. I tried making flash cards for the first time and they were cool.

www.channel4.com/homework/index.jsp

Click on **Science**.

Homework High is a great website to help you in particular with homework. You can type in a question, get answers or visit the library for information. You can access other subjects too. There are timetabled slots for live chats so your questions can be answered immediately.

Use **The Library** to answer most questions.

Great for all subjects.

www.kids.net.au

Click 
, Chemistry, 
, 
.

Play the game of hangman to learn the names of the elements. Use the other two options for other quizzes to help revise for SATs.

Play with a friend to help each other get the names and the symbols correct.

www.chemicool.com

An easy way to revise.

www.bgfl.org

Click on **Pupils 11–16**, then on **KS3**, **Learning Zone**, **Science** and **Measures**.

This is a good site for general measurements and maths.

Test yourself and really have a go at improving your confidence in maths.

This was maths, but I think it helps for revising science too.

www.physics.org

Click on **Physics Life** then click the area you wish to explore.

This website gives you the Physics behind everyday objects, such as telephones, lifts, fuses and computers.

Clicking the red words gives you detailed explanations of the Physics behind the object.

Takes a long time to load. It's good to look at the Physics that's in the things you see every day.

www.bbc.co.uk/schools

Click on **KS3 Bitesize** in the *Revision Guide* section, choose **Science** then **Physics**.

This excellent and easy-to-use site enables you to choose your own level of work. Choose either Levels 5–6 or Level 7 **Electricity And Magnetism**.

.

Revise the topic then **Test** yourself.

www.zephyrus.co.uk
The Physics section of this site is packed with all the info you need for your SATs.

Its good because you can test yourself and if you get anything wrong you can revise it.

www.scienceyear.com

Click **Get Gaming** from the main menu. Apparently, 'you'll never leave your seat again'!

Science-based computer games.

Use **Climbin' High** for rock cycle revision, **Planet 10** for solar systems revision and **Teacher's Pet** for a laugh!

Takes a long time to load, but the games are good.

www.wsu.edu/DrUniverse

Simply click on **How Do I Submit My Questions?**.

Why do your hands go wrinkly in water? What gas is found in chilli peppers? Are primates either right or left-handed like us? Ask Dr Universe your impossible questions and get the brains at Washington State University to do the work for you!

This should be your last resort! Try to find the answer yourself by looking at the other sites recommended in this book.

www.sciencemuseum.org.uk

Click on **Exhibitions Online** and **Exploring Leonardo**.

There is a lot of information about Leonardo da Vinci. Try navigating around the site and look at his inventions and his artwork.

Look at his use of colours and then what he did in Physics for diving and flight.

I liked this site. Leonardo was clever and his pictures were bright.

Published by Letts Educational
The Chiswick Centre
414 Chiswick High Road
London W4 5TF
Tel: 020 89963333
Fax: 020 87428390
E-mail: mail@lettsed.co.uk
Web: www.letts-education.com

Letts Educational is part of the Granada Learning Group. Granada Learning is a division of Granada plc.

First published 2004

ISBN 1844190331

British Library Cataloguing in Publication Data
A catalogue record for this book is available from the British Library.

Commissioned by Helen Clark
Project management by Julia Swales
Editing by Vicky Butt
Original cover and internal design by Gecko, Bicester
Page layout and management by Bigtop Design, Bicester
Production by PDQ
Printed and bound by Canale